FROM **DIXIE** TO **SWING**

To access audio visit:
www.halleonard.com/mylibrary

4784-6823-5728-9883

ISBN 978-1-59615-261-8

EXCLUSIVELY DISTRIBUTED BY

7777 W. BLUEMOUND RD. P.O. BOX 13819 MILWAUKEE, WI 53213

Visit Hal Leonard Online at
www.halleonard.com

CONTENTS

Way Down Yonder In New Orleans

CLARINET &
SOPRANO SAX

Words and Music by
HENRY CREAMER
J. TURNER LAYTON

There is Heav - en right here on earth__ With those beau - ti - ful queens,
They've got an - gels right here on earth__ Wear - ing lit - tle blue jeans,

'Way down yon - der in New Or - leans.

5

Red Sails In The Sunset

Words and Music by
JIMMY KENNEDY
HUGH WILLIAMS
(WILL GROSZ)

CLARINET &
SOPRANO SAX

7

Second Hand Rose

Words and Music by
GRANT CLARKE
JAMES F. HANLEY

CLARINET &
SOPRANO SAX

Take 4 bars rest,
Then repeat last 4 bars

Royal Garden Blues

Rose Of Washington Square

13

build to end

On The Sunny Side Of The Street

Words and Music by
DOROTHY FIELD
JIMMY McHUGH

I Want A Little Girl

Exactly Like You

CLARINET &
SOPRANO SAX

Words and Music by
DOROTHY FIELDS
JIMMY McHUGH

ADVANCED ALTO SAX SOLOS – VOLUME 1
Performed by Paul Brodie, alto saxophone
Accompaniment: Antonin Kubalek, piano

Virtuoso Paul Brodie introduces you to the world of advanced alto sax solos with this wide-ranging collection. Contains performance suggestions and Mr. Brodie's incredible interpretations to help you achieve greatness! Includes a printed music score containing the solo part, annotated with performance suggestions; and access to professional recordings with complete versions (with soloist) followed by piano accompaniments to each piece, minus the soloist. Includes works by Vivaldi, Jacob, Whitney, and Benson.

00400602 Book/Online Audio......................$14.99

ADVANCED ALTO SAX SOLOS – VOLUME 2
Performed by Vincent Abato, alto saxophone
Accompaniment: Harriet Wingreen, piano

Listen as extraordinary virtuoso Vincent Abato of the Metropolitan Opera Orchestra takes you further into the advanced repertoire with these spectacular sax selections. Listen to his masterful interpretations, examine his performance suggestions, then you step in and make magic with Harriet Wingreen, legendary piano accompanist for the New York Philharmonic. Includes: Schubert "The Bee," Rabaud "Solo de Concours," and Creston "Sonata, Op. 19" 2nd and 3rd movements. Includes a printed music score containing the solo part, annotated with performance suggestions; and tracks with complete versions (with soloist) followed by piano accompaniments to each piece, minus the soloist.

00400603 Book/Online Audio $14.99

PLAY THE MUSIC OF BURT BACHARACH
ALTO OR TENOR SAXOPHONE

Along with lyricist Hal David, Burt Bacharach penned some of the best pop songs and standards of all time. These superb collections let solo instrumentalists play along with: Alfie • Blue on Blue • Do You Know the Way to San Jose • I Say a Little Prayer • Magic Moments • This Guy's in Love with You • Walk on By • What the World Needs Now • The Windows of the World • and Wives and Lovers.

00400657 Book/Online Audio $19.99

BOSSA, BONFÁ & BLACK ORPHEUS FOR TENOR SAXOPHONE – A TRIBUTE TO STAN GETZ
TENOR SAXOPHONE
featuring Glenn Zottola

Original transcriptions for you to perform! The bossa novas that swept the world in 1950 created a whole new set of songs to equal the great standards of the '20s, '30s and '40s by Gershwin, Porter, Arlen, Berlin, Kern and Rodgers. This collection for tenor sax is a tribute to the great Stan Getz and includes: Black Orpheus • Girl from Ipanema • Gentle Rain • One Note Samba • Once I Loved • Dindi • Baubles, Bangles and Beads • Meditation • Triste • I Concentrate on You • Samba de Orfeu.

00124387 Book/Online Audio.....................................$14.99

CLASSIC STANDARDS FOR ALTO SAXOPHONE
A TRIBUTE TO JOHNNY HODGES
featuring Bob Wilber

Ten classic standards are presented in this book as they were arranged for the Neal Hefti String Orchestra in 1954, including: Yesterdays • Laura • What's New? • Blue Moon • Can't Help Lovin' Dat Man • Embraceable You • Willow Weep for Me • Memories of You • Smoke Gets in Your Eyes • Stardust. Bob Wilber performs the songs on the provided CD on soprano saxophone, although they are translated for alto saxophone.

00131389 Book/CD Pack....................................$14.99

EASY JAZZ DUETS FOR 2 ALTO SAXOPHONES AND RHYTHM SECTION
Performed by Hal McKusick, alto saxophone
Accompaniment: The Benny Goodman Rhythm Section: George Duvivier, bass; Bobby Donaldson, drums

This great collection of jazz duets gives you the opportunity accompany saxophonist Hal McKusick and the Benny Goodma Rhythm Section. Suitable for beginning players, all the selectio are great fun. This album allows you to play either duet par Includes printed musical score with access to online audio track you hear both parts played in stereo, then each duet is repeat with the first part omitted and then the second part, so you can play along.

00400480 Book/Online Audio..................................$14.9

FROM DIXIE TO SWING
CLARINET OR SOPRANO SAX
Performed by Kenny Davern, clarinet
Accompaniment: Kenny Davern, clarinet & soprano sax; 'Doc' Cheatham, trumpet; Vic Dickenson, trombone; Dick Wellstoo piano; George Duvivier, bass; Gus Johnson Jr., drums

Such jazz legends as Dick Wellstood, Alphonse 'Doc' Cheatham an George Duvivier and more back you up in this amazing collectio of New York-style Dixieland standards. After the break-up of th big-band era around 1950, many of the finest 'swing' or main stream players found themselves without an outlet for their abilitie and took to playing 'Dixieland' in New York clubs such as Eddie Condon's and the Metropole And so was born a new style of Dixieland jazz minus the banjos, tubas, steamboats and mag nolias! It is this version we celebrate on this album. We encourage you, the soloist, to inven counter-melodies rather than mere harmony parts. This is a music of loose weaving parts, no one of precision ensemble figures. And in short, it is one of the greatest improvisational expe riences any jazz player could hope to have. Includes a printed music score and online audi access to stereo accompaniments to each piece.

00400613 Book/Online Audio $14.99

GLAZUNOV – CONCERTO IN E-FLAT MAJOR, OP. 109; VON KOCH – CONCERTO IN E-FLAT MAJOR
ALTO SAXOPHONE
Performed by Lawrence Gwozdz, alto saxophone
Accompaniment: Plovdiv Philharmonic Orchestra
Conductor: Nayden Todorov

Alexander Glazunov, one of the great masters of late Russian Romanticism, was fascinated by the saxophone and by jazz. In 1934 he wrote this beautiful saxophone concerto which has become a classic, combining romanticism with modern idioms as well. Erland von Koch's 1958 saxophone concerto is filled with experimental modern tonalities and fantastic effects for the saxophone. Both are must-haves for the serious saxophonist. Includes a printed music score; informative liner notes; and online audio featuring the concerti performed twice: first with soloist, then again with orchestral accompaniment only, minus you, the soloist. The audio is accessed online using the unique code inside each book and can be streamed or downloaded.

00400487 Book/Online Audio..................................$14.99

To see a full listing of Music Minus One publications, visit
www.halleonard.com/MusicMinusOne